A Kalmus Classic Edit

Johannes

BRAHMS

PIANO PIECES

Opus 119

Edited by
E. V. SAUER

FOR PIANO

K 03259

Piano Pieces

Intermezzo.

Op. 119 Nº 1. (1893)

Adagio.

Intermezzo.

Andantino un poco agitato.

Op. 119 № 2.

Andantino grazioso.

Intermezzo.

Op. 119 N<u>o</u> 3.

Rhapsody

Op. 119 №. 4.

Allegro risoluto.